Contents

Minted Lime Scallops	2
Sea Scallops With Shallots And Walnuts	2
Scallops Hampton	2
Fried Virginia Oysters With Collard Slaw And Creme Fraiche	5
Grilled Oyster Brochettes	5
Eastern Shore Oysters With Wild Mushrooms, Fresh Herbs And Lobster Butter	6
Oysters Bingo	6
Summer Oyster Salad	7
Grilled Clams With Papaya-Red Pepper Salsa	7
Clams With Red Peppers And Pasta	9
Oven-Cooked Clams	9
Clam Corn Chowder	9
Sautéed Soft-Shell Crabs With Cucumber, Ham And Shiitake Mushrooms With Herb Butter	10
Grilled Soft-Shells With Ginger Lime Sauce And Shallots	10
Soft-Shell Crab Stack	12
Virginia Soft-Shell Crabs With Lemon Butter And Almonds	12
Soft-Shell Crab Imperial	13
Boiled Spiced Crabs	13
Crab, Orange and Avocado Salad	13
Chesapeake Bay Blue Crab Cakes	15
Tartar Sauce	15
Cocktail Sauce From Hell	15
Dill-Dijon Butter	15
Crab Cakes Lynnhaven Inlet	16
Eastern Shore Jumbo Crabmeat With Local Asparagus And Cilantro Mustard Sauce	16
Virginia Ham And Blue Crab Chowder	17
Tomato Angel Hair Pasta With Jumbo Lump Crabmeat	17
Smithfield Backfin Crab Rollup With James River Sauce	18
Virginia Waterfront Blue Crab Feast	18
Norfolk Crabmeat In Butter	18
Pirates Style Fish Stew	19
Crispy Fried Shad Roe With Mirepoix Of Tomato, Onion, Provence Olives And Lemon Zest	19
Pepper Seared Tuna Filled With Goats' Cheese, Tomatoes, Mushrooms, Basil And Garlic	20
Pan Seared Tuna With Curry Dipping Sauce	20
Sautéed Fresh Tuna Medallion Oriental	22
Rockfish On Bed Of Leeks	22
Horeseradish-Crusted Rockfish	22
Barbecued Bluefish	23
Smokey Marinated Mackerel	23
Grilled Taylor Blues With Fresh Corn Salsa	25
Cedar Planked Sea Trout On Fresh Shiitake Mushrooms With Tomato-Basil Compote	25
Potato Chip Encrusted Striped Bass With Sautéed Backfin Crab, Papaya And Fresh Pineapple	26
Sea Trout Norfolk	26
Steamed Black Sea Bass	28
Mahi Mahi With Christo Sauce	28
Flounder Baked In Parchment With Tomatoes, Red Onion, Garlic, Lemon Zest And Rosemary	29
Ocean View Flounder	29
Grilled Oriental Croaker/Spot	31
Spicy Pan-Fried Croaker	31
Virginia Croaker With Brown Potatoes And Sausage Butter	31

We dedicate this book, with gratitude, to the many excellent Virginia Waterfront chefs who donated recipes to this cookbook and showed us how to make the best of this great natural resource.

The sea scallop shell can grow as large as eight inches in diameter. The edible part of the scallop can reach two inches in diameter.

Minted Lime Scallops

1¼ pounds sea scallops	½ teaspoon salt
1 clove garlic, minced	½ teaspoon pepper, freshly ground
1 tablespoon vegetable oil	⅛ - ¼ teaspoon cayenne pepper
¼ cup water	¼ cup fresh mint, chopped
¼ cup lime juice	1 ripe avocado, diced
¼ cup green onions, finely chopped	Bibb or Boston lettuce
1 teaspoon grated lime zest*	

In a covered saucepan, gently poach scallops with garlic, vegetable oil and water for 3 to 4 minutes, turning once. Using a slotted spoon, remove scallops to a ceramic or glass bowl. Rapidly boil down liquid in a pan to about ¼ cup. Cool and combine this liquid with remaining ingredients, except avocado and lettuce. Pour over scallops in bowl. Refrigerate for 1 to 2 hours. Just before serving, peel and dice avocado. Toss gently with the scallops. Serve on lettuce garnished with additional mint sprigs. Serves 4. Pictured at right.

* The zest is the colored part of the citrus peel with none of the bitter white membrane.

Total calories per serving: 369 • Percentage of calories from protein: 32 • Percentage of calories from carbohydrates: 10
Percentage of calories from fat: 56 • Percentage of calories from saturated fat: 8

Virginia is one of the largest producers of sea scallops in the nation.

Sea Scallops With Shallots And Walnuts

2 pounds sea scallops, patted dry	¾ cup toasted walnuts, coarsely chopped
6 tablespoons unsalted butter	4 teaspoons chives, finely chopped
4 tablespoons light olive oil	salt
4 teaspoons shallots, pared, finely chopped	white pepper

Heat butter and oil over medium heat until hot. Add scallops and sauté for 2 to 3 minutes, then add shallots and stir. Add walnuts and chives and cook for 1 minute; drain off excess fat. • Season to taste with salt and pepper. • Divide onto four warm serving plates and garnish with lemon wedges. *Serves 4 to 6.*

Based upon 6 servings
Total calories per serving: 555 • Percentage of calories from protein: 24 • Percentage of calories from carbohydrates: 7
Percentage of calories from fat: 68 • Percentage of calories from saturated fat: 17

Seafood is very low in calories. 3.5 ounces of a low-fat fish such as flounder contains 80 calories, while a high-fat fish such as bluefish is just 139.

Scallops Hampton
Chef Michael Drury, Radisson Hotel, Hampton

1 tablespoon olive oil	1 pinch ground black pepper
1 tablespoon garlic, finely chopped	1 pinch granulated onion
¼ cup white wine	1 pinch celery salt
1 tablespoon lemon juice	2 tablespoons fresh parsley, chopped
12 ounces large sea scallops	2 tablespoons whole butter
⅓ cup chicken broth	1 puff pastry
1 pinch Hungarian paprika	

In a sauté pan, heat the olive oil. Add the chopped garlic and sauté until garlic is lightly browned. Add white wine, lemon juice and scallops and sauté. When wine reduces to half its volume, add chicken broth and poach scallops until cooked. Finish sauce with seasonings and herbs. Stir in whole butter a little at a time to complete sauce. • Cut out a 3½-inch round of puff pastry. Bake in 375 degree oven until it rises and is lightly browned. • Serve on a puff pastry shell. *Serves 4.*

Total calories per serving: 274 • Percentage of calories from protein: 38 • Percentage of calories from carbohydrates: 6
Percentage of calories from fat: 48 • Percentage of calories from saturated fat: 16

Fried Virginia Oysters With Collard Slaw and Creme Fraiche

Chef/Owner Sydney Meers, The Dumbwaiter Bistro, Norfolk

1½ pints shucked oysters
1 cup cornmeal
2 cups flour
  pinch salt and pepper
  peanut oil for frying

Mix meal, flour and seasonings together for dredge.

Collard Slaw

6 collard leaves, cut into chiffanode*
½ head white cabbage, shredded
½ cup mayonnaise
2 tablespoons black seedy mustard
2 tablespoons white vinegar
2 tablespoons sugar
  pinch salt and pepper

Mix this together and let set in refrigerator at least 1 hour.
*Cut into ribbons.

Creme Fraiche

1 cup sour cream
2 ounces buttermilk
½ ounce fresh orange juice

Mix all together and let stand overnight.

To assemble: Toss oysters in the dredge to coat them lightly and fry them in hot peanut oil quickly so as to get crisp on the outside and still moist inside. Place on the slaw and place the creme fraiche on the side. Serve with pickled okra and deviled eggs.

Serves 6. Pictured at left.

Total calories per serving: 407
Percentage of calories from protein: 7
Percentage of calories from carbohydrates: 16
Percentage of calories from fat: 75
Percentage of calories from saturated fat: 29

Seafood is the quick answer for today's busy cook. Almost every variety of seafood lends itself to microwaving. Plan on about 4 to 5 minutes per pound. Be careful not to overcook.

Grilled Oyster Brochettes

16 oysters
1 teaspoon lemon juice
  spice mixture (¼ - ½ teaspoon)
16 mushroom caps
4 strips bacon
1 red or green bell pepper, cut into 1-inch pieces
3 teaspoons butter
2 teaspoons chopped parsley
4 lemon wedges *(optional)*

Spice mixture: Combine 1 teaspoon salt, ¼ teaspoon freshly ground black pepper, ¼ ground white pepper, ¼ ground red pepper and ½ teaspoon dried oregano (enough for 4 brochettes). • Drain oysters and sprinkle with lemon juice and the spice mixture. Using a skewer, place a mushroom cap on the end, then the end of the bacon strip, then the pepper square, then an oyster, then wrap the bacon around the oyster and pepper and onto the skewer again. Continue alternating as above. Brush with butter and broil over charcoal for 4 to 6 minutes, turning twice. Sprinkle with parsley and serve with lemon wedge if desired. *Serves 4.*

Note: Cooked brochettes can be served on frankfurter buns if desired. Brochettes may also be broiled in oven about 4 inches from heat 5 to 7 minutes.

Total calories per serving: 129 • Percentage of calories from protein: 24 • Percentage of calories from carbohydrates: 18
Percentage of calories from fat: 56 • Percentage of calories from saturated fat: 22

When buying live oysters or clams, make sure that the shell is tightly closed - or that it closes easily when handled. Discard any with gaping shells since they are dead and inedible.

Eastern Shore Oysters With Wild Mushrooms, Fresh Herbs And Lobster Butter

Chef Marcel Desaulniers, The Trellis, Williamsburg

2 pints Eastern Shore oysters, shucked	salt and pepper, to taste
assorted fresh herbs	2 tablespoons dry white wine
1 live lobster, 2½ - 3 pounds	½ pound sliced wild mushrooms, stems
1 teaspoon salt	trimmed or removed as necessary
½ pound unsalted butter, softened	

Remove the tail and claws from the lobster body. Cook the tail and claws in 3 quarts of boiling water, salted with 1 teaspoon of salt, for 10 minutes. During this cooking time, cut the lobster body into 1- to 1½-inch pieces. • Remove the lobster tail and claws from cooking water. Rinse under running cold water until cool enough to handle. Remove the meat from tail and claws. • Return the broken tail and claw shells to the cooking water along with the cut up body pieces. Allow this mixture to come to a simmer over medium heat. Cut the cooked tail and claw meat into ¼-inch pieces, cover with film wrap and refrigerate until needed. • Simmer the lobster shells for 3 hours. Drain the shells in a colander, reserving the stock, pushing down on the shells to extract as much stock as possible. Return stock (about 3 cups) to the saucepan and allow to simmer for 1 hour. Strain stock into a non-stick sauté pan and reduce over low heat to 2 tablespoons, about 20 minutes. • In a food processor fitted with a metal blade, process the butter, lobster meat and lobster stock reduction until smooth. Season with salt and pepper and combine thoroughly. Cover with plastic wrap and refrigerate until ready to use. • Heat 2 tablespoons of lobster butter and white wine in a large non-stick sauté pan over medium-high heat. When the mixture comes to a full boil, add the sliced wild mushrooms, lightly season with salt and pepper, and sauté for 1½ to 2 minutes. • Add the oysters, lightly season with salt and pepper and heat at a simmer (adjust heat if necessary) until the edges of the oysters begin to curl, 4 to 5 minutes. Add the remaining lobster butter and simmer for an additional minute or two. • Portion the oyster mixture into each of 4 individual warm soup plates. Garnish with fresh herbs and serve immediately. *Serves 4.*

Total calories per serving: 570 • Percentage of calories from protein: 14 • Percentage of calories from carbohydrates: 5
Percentage of calories from fat: 79 • Percentage of calories from saturated fat: 47

Oysters Bingo

Proprietor Joe Hoggard and Chef Bobby Huber, Jr., The Ships Cabin, Norfolk

1 cup flour	1 tablespoon oyster juice
salt and pepper to taste	1 tablespoon lemon juice
6 fresh oysters	1 tablespoon shallots
2 tablespoons butter	6 oyster shells, cleaned
1 tablespoon white wine	

Combine flour with salt and pepper. Lightly coat oysters in flour. Sauté in butter until golden brown. Remove from pan. *To make sauce:* remove pan from heat and add the wine, oyster juice, lemon juice and shallots to the butter in the pan. Place each oyster in a shell and pour sauce over it Serve hot. *Serves 1 to 2.*

Based upon 2 servings
Total calories per serving: 201 • Percentage of calories from protein: 7 • Percentage of calories from carbohydrates: 7
Percentage of calories from fat: 82 • Percentage of calories from saturated fat: 49

Summer Oyster Salad

8 ounces spaghettini or other pasta	1 clove garlic, minced *or* ⅛ teaspoon garlic powder
1 pint oysters	½ teaspoon salt
1 tablespoon lemon juice	¼ teaspoon freshly ground black pepper
½ cup sliced green onions	⅛ teaspoon ground red pepper
1 large tomato, seeded and diced	½ cup grated Parmesan cheese
½ cup olive oil	½ pound bacon, cooked and crumbled *(optional)*
¼ cup lemon juice	

Cook pasta according to package directions. Poach oysters in their own liquid to which 1 tablespoon lemon juice has been added. Cook about 5 minutes or until oysters just begin to curl. Do not overcook. Cool. Drain, reserving ½ cup of the broth. Cut oysters in thirds or halves. In a small bowl, combine olive oil, lemon juice, garlic, salt, pepper, red pepper and the ½ cup of reserved oyster liquid. In a large bowl, lightly toss pasta, oysters and dressing. Chill thoroughly. Just before serving, add Parmesan cheese and toss lightly. Top with crumbled bacon if desired. *Serves 4.*

With bacon - Total calories per serving: 652 • Percentage of calories from protein: 15 • Percentage of calories from carbohydrates: 14 • Percentage of calories from fat: 69 • Percentage of calories from saturated fat: 19

Without bacon - Total calories per serving: 488 • Percentage of calories from protein: 14 • Percentage of calories from carbohydrates: 18 • Percentage of calories from fat: 67 • Percentage of calories from saturated fat: 17

Lots of people think that oysters can be eaten only during months that have an "R." But that's an old folk tale from the days of poor refrigeration. So go ahead and enjoy them year-round.

Grilled Clams With Papaya-Red Pepper Salsa

1 small ripe papaya (about 14 ounces), peeled, seeded and finely diced	4 pounds live hard-shell Virginia clams (cherrystone or little neck)
2 tablespoons lime juice	1 large red bell pepper, stemmed, seeded and quartered lengthwise *or* ½ of a 7-ounce jar of roasted red peppers, drained and diced
1-2 tablespoons minced fresh cilantro sprigs	
2 teaspoons firmly packed brown sugar	
¼ teaspoon dry hot red chili flakes	

While briquets are heating: In a bowl combine papaya, lime juice, cilantro, brown sugar and chili flakes (plus diced peppers, if using bottled peppers); set aside. • Scrub clams under cool running water. Discard any that either are not firmly closed, or do not pull shut when rinsed (it's okay if they reopen upon sitting). • *To grill:* If using fresh bell pepper, add 10 to 12 additional fresh briquets to the bed of hot coals just before cooking (these will be hot when it is time to add the clams). Place pepper wedges skin side down on an oiled grill over hot coals. Cook until skin is mostly black, 8 to 10 minutes. Remove pepper from grill and peel off loose skin (not all skin needs to come off). Finely dice pepper and stir into salsa. • Meanwhile, place clams on grill and cook until they pop wide open, 5 to 12 minutes. • *To serve:* Transfer open clams to a serving dish. Discard any that do not open. To eat, break off top shell, loosen clam in shell, spoon salsa on top and enjoy! *Makes 8 to 12 appetizer servings or 4 to 6 main dish servings.*

Based upon 4 main dish servings
Total calories per serving: 91 • Percentage of calories from protein: 43 • Percentage of calories from carbohydrates: 46 Percentage of calories from fat: 10 • Percentage of calories from saturated fat: 1

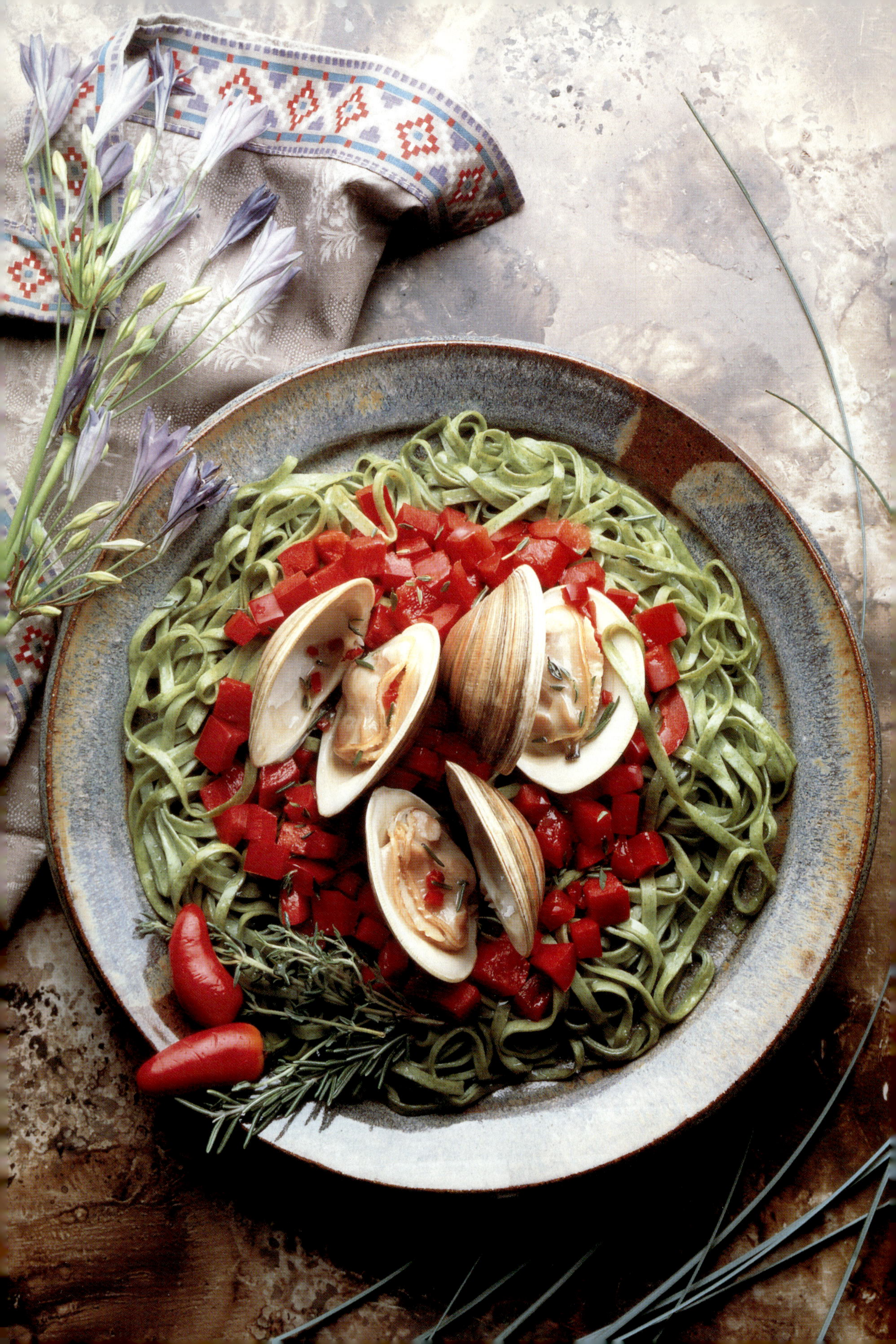

Clams With Red Peppers And Pasta

- 3 dozen littleneck or cherrystone clams
- ¼ cup vinegar
- 2 tablespoons olive oil
- 2 tablespoons butter
- 1 clove garlic, minced
- 1 hot red chili pepper, minced or cayenne to taste
- 2 large red bell peppers, seeded and diced
- ½ teaspoon fresh rosemary, chopped
- ½ teaspoon fresh thyme leaves
- ½ teaspoon salt
- ¼ teaspoon pepper
- 8 ounces green linguine or other pasta

Scrub clams, cover them with water and vinegar. Let stand 30 minutes, drain and rinse. Prepare pasta according to package directions so that completion coincides with rest of preparation. Heat oil and butter in a skillet. Add garlic and hot pepper. Sauté gently about 1 minute. Stir in remaining ingredients and clams. Cover and simmer 4 minutes or until clams open. Serve over cooked linguine. *Serves 4. Pictured at left.*

Total calories per serving: 368 • Percentage of calories from protein: 33 • Percentage of calories from carbohydrates: 27 Percentage of calories from fat: 38 • Percentage of calories from saturated fat: 12

Oven-Cooked Clams

Chef Ray Olivio, Keith's Dockside, Hampton

- 24 select little neck clams
- ½ cup olive oil
- seasoned breadcrumbs
- parsley, chopped
- 1 teaspoon garlic, chopped
- salt and pepper, to taste
- Parmesan cheese, to taste
- lemon wedges for garnish

Wash the clams. Clean, scrape and open them, reserving their natural juices. Place under running water to remove any traces of sand and pieces of shells. • Place the half shells containing clams on an oven-proof dish. Season the clams with breadcrumbs, parsley, garlic, salt and pepper. • Sprinkle the clams with their natural juices and the olive oil. • Preheat oven to 375 degrees. Bake for 10 to 12 minutes. Serve as soon as the clams are ready, with lemon wedges and grated Parmesan cheese on the side. *Serves 4.*

Total calories per serving: 325 • Percentage of calories from protein: 14 • Percentage of calories from carbohydrates: 4 Percentage of calories from fat: 81 • Percentage of calories from saturated fat: 13

Clam Corn Chowder

- 1 quart whole fresh shucked clams or 2 (7-ounce) cans minced clams
- water as needed
- 3 slices bacon, chopped
- 1 cup onion, chopped
- 2 cups raw potatoes, diced
- 1½ cups whole-kernel corn, drained
- 3 cups milk
- 2 tablespoons flour
- 1 tablespoon butter or margarine
- 1 teaspoon celery salt
- 1 teaspoon salt
- dash of pepper
- ½ cup coarse cracker crumbs *(optional)*

Chop whole clams or drain canned clams. Reserve liquid. Pour clam liquid into measuring cup and add water as needed to fill to 1 cup level. In a large pot, fry bacon until crisp; add onion and cook until tender. Add potatoes, clam liquid, and water. Cover; simmer gently until potatoes are tender. Add corn and milk. Blend flour and butter or margarine and stir into soup. Cook slowly until mixture thickens slightly, stirring constantly. Add seasoning and clams; simmer 5 minutes. Top with cracker crumbs. Serve hot. *Serves 6.*

Total calories per serving: 364 • Percentage of calories from protein: 21 • Percentage of calories from carbohydrates: 52 Percentage of calories from fat: 25 • Percentage of calories from saturated fat: 12

Clam size varies according to grade:
Chowders -
3½ inches in width
Cherrystones -
2½ to 3½ inches
Top Necks -
2½ inches
Little Necks -
1½ to 2½ inches

Also commonly known as the "quahog", the clam was first used for barter as a form of money or "wampum". It was probably valued above other shells because of the dark purple inside the shell.

Clam meat is low in calories. 3.5 ounces have 74 calories, 12.8% protein and .6% fat.

In Virginia, soft-shells generally appear around the first full moon of May. They will be available fresh until September or early October. After that they are available frozen year-round.

Sautéed Soft-Shell Crabs With Julienne Of Cucumber, Country Ham And Shiitake Mushrooms With Herb Butter

Chef Marcel Desaulniers, The Trellis, Williamsburg

12 soft-shell blue crabs, cleaned
4 tablespoons lemon juice
   salt and pepper, to taste
½ cup all-purpose flour
   (seasoned with salt and pepper)
6 tablespoons unsalted butter
6 cucumbers, peeled, seeded and cut lengthwise into long thin strips
½ pound shiitake mushrooms, sliced
¼ pound country ham, cut in julienne
Herb Butter Sauce

Herb Butter Sauce

1 tablespoon all-purpose flour
1 tablespoon butter, softened
¼ cup fish stock
¼ cup white wine
¼ cup unsalted butter
1 tablespoon fresh herbs, chopped
   salt and pepper, to taste

Combine flour and softened butter until mixture is smooth and free of lumps. In a small pan, heat fish stock and white wine to a boil. Quickly whip butter and flour mixture into boiling hot stock and wine. Remove pan from heat. Whip whole butter into thickened mixture 1 tablespoon at a time. When all the butter has been incorporated into the sauce, add the chopped herbs. Season with salt and pepper, to taste. Hold away from heat until served.

Sprinkle lemon juice over soft-shells, season with salt and pepper. Cover and refrigerate until ready to cook. • Pat crabs dry with paper towel. Dust with flour using up to ½ cup, as necessary. Heat 2 tablespoons of butter in large sauté pan. When butter is hot, carefully sauté crabs, shell side first, until golden brown on both sides. Remove crabs from pan and hold warm. • In a clean sauté pan, sauté cucumbers in 2 tablespoons of butter. In a separate pan, sauté shiitake mushrooms and country ham in 2 tablespoons of butter. When all the ingredients are hot, assemble dish. • *To assemble:* Place cucumbers on the base of individual dinner plates (divide evenly). Portion 2 to 3 tablespoons of herb butter sauce over each plate of cucumbers. Set soft-shell crabs on top of cucumbers (2 per plate). Finish by spooning shiitake and ham mixture over the crabs (divide evenly). Serve immediately. Serves 6. Pictured at right.

Total calories per serving: 579
Percentage of calories from protein: 22
Percentage of calories from carbohydrates: 19
Percentage of calories from fat: 57
Percentage of calories from saturated fat: 19

Grilled Soft-Shells With Ginger Lime Sauce And Shallots

12 large soft-shell crabs, dressed
8 tablespoons unsalted butter, clarified
1 lime zest* and 2 tablespoons juice
2 teaspoons fresh ginger, grated
   salt, to taste
1 shallot, finely chopped

Prepare a medium-hot charcoal fire and set cooking grid 5 to 6 inches above coals. • In a small pan, mix butter, lime zest, juice, shallot and ginger. Taste and add salt if desired. Keep sauce warm while crabs are grilling. • Brush each crab with sauce and grill, turning once, 5 to 7 minutes on each side, depending on thickness. (Crabs are done when they turn rich red-brown and back feeler legs are crisp.) Place crabs on heated serving platter and cover with remaining sauce. Serves 6.

* *The zest is the colored part of the citrus peel with none of the bitter white membrane.*

Total calories per serving: 252 • Percentage of calories from protein: 24 • Percentage of calories from carbohydrates: 22
Percentage of calories from fat: 53 • Percentage of calories from saturated fat: 13

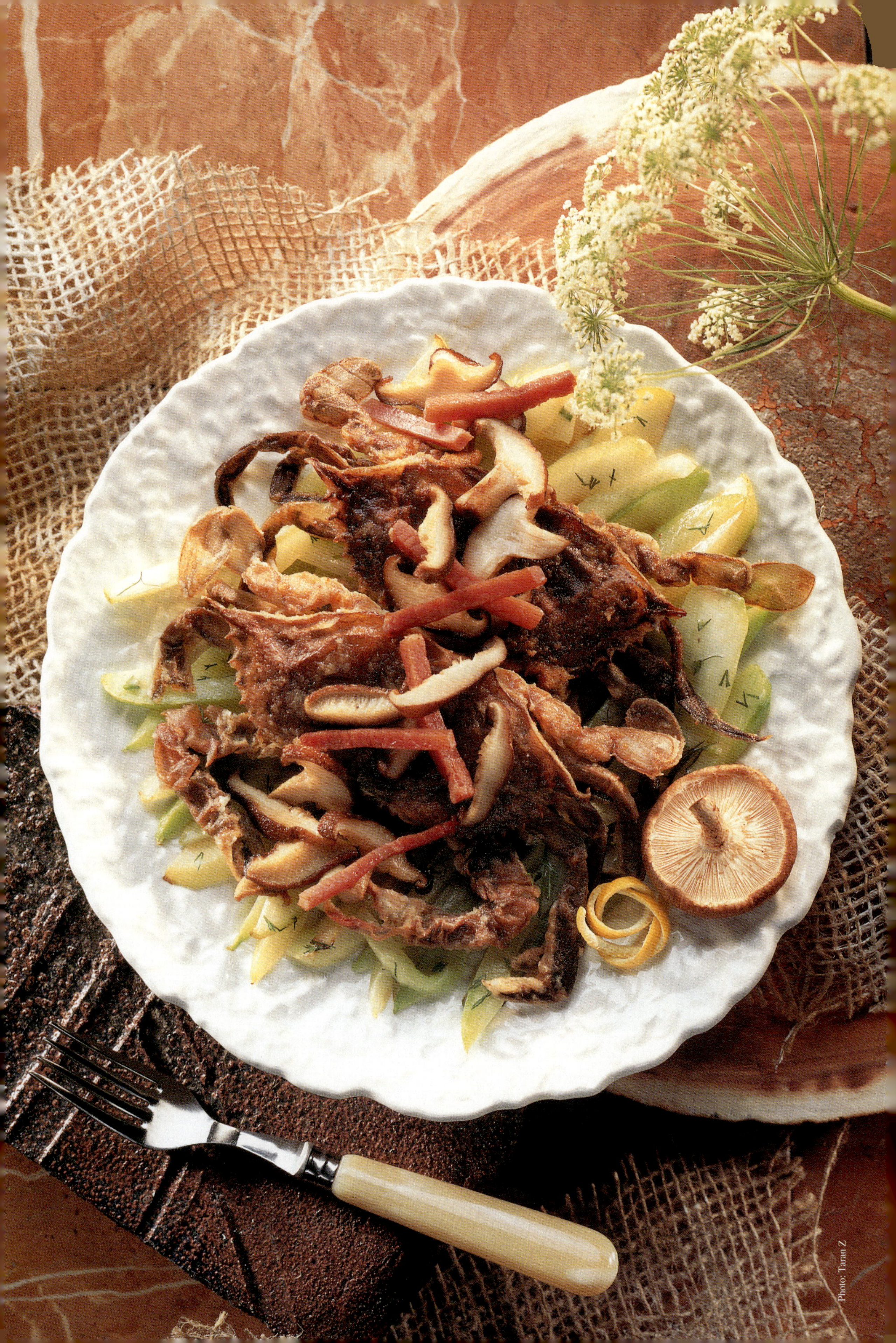
Photo: Taran Z

Soft-shells are marketed by size with the largest commanding the premium prices. Crabs are measured across the back, point-to-point. "Mediums" are 3½ to 4 inches; "Hotels" are 4 to 4½ inches; "Primes" are 4½ to 5 inches; "Jumbos" are 5 to 5½ inches and "Whales" are over 5½ inches.

Soft-Shell Crab Stack

8 soft-shell crabs, cleaned
3 tablespoons butter
4 English muffins, split, toasted and buttered
8 slices cooked ham, ⅛- to ¼-inch thick
8 slices ripe tomato
1½-1¾ cups hollandaise sauce

Prick legs and claws of each crab with the tines of a fork to prevent popping. Sauté in butter about 4 minutes on each side over moderate heat. • *To assemble:* Place toasted English muffin halves on plate. Top each with ham, then tomato and cooked crab. Spoon about 3 tablespoons hollandaise sauce over each. Serve immediately. *Serves 4.*

Hollandaise Sauce

4 egg yolks
3 tablespoons lemon juice
¼ teaspoon salt
¼ teaspoon white pepper
⅛ teaspoon cayenne pepper
1 cup butter

Place egg yolks, lemon juice and seasonings in a blender. At medium speed, very slowly add 1 cup butter which has been melted to bubbling but not browned. Blend an additional 10 to 12 seconds until sauce is thickened and smooth.

Total calories per serving: 661 • Percentage of calories from protein: 22 • Percentage of calories from carbohydrates: 16 Percentage of calories from fat: 60 • Percentage of calories from saturated fat: 32

Virginia Soft-Shell Crabs With Lemon Butter And Almonds

1 dozen soft-shell crabs, cleaned
2 cups flour
½ stick butter
½ cup dry white wine
   juice of 1 medium lemon
1 teaspoon shallots, chopped
¼ cup heavy cream
1 stick unsalted butter, cut in pieces
3 ounces sliced almonds, toasted

Pat dry soft-shell crabs with paper towel and dust in flour. • Heat large 12-inch skillet over medium heat until hot. Add 2 pats of butter to skillet. Place 4 crabs in skillet, shell side down. Sauté until brown, 3 minutes. Turn over with spatula and cook until brown. Add more butter if necessary. Repeat for other crabs. • When complete, keep crabs on warm platter or oven until service. Drain skillet of any excess oil, then add wine, shallots and lemon juice to skillet. Reduce by ⅔ volume over medium heat. Slowly add heavy cream while stirring. Reduce and bring to a simmer. When thickened, reduce heat and add cut pieces of butter. Whip smooth until blended. • *To assemble:* Place 3 soft-shell crabs shellside up on plate. Pour 4 tablespoons of lemon butter sauce over crabs. Garnish with 2 tablespoons of toasted sliced almonds. *Serves 4*.

Total calories per serving: 635 • Percentage of calories from protein: 24 • Percentage of calories from carbohydrates: 4 Percentage of calories from fat: 70 • Percentage of calories from saturated fat: 31

Soft-Shell Crab Imperial

¼ cup butter
2 tablespoons flour
1 cup milk
2 teaspoons prepared mustard
½ teaspoon salt
⅛-¼ teaspoon red pepper
1 pound backfin crabmeat
3 tablespoons butter, melted
12 soft-shell crabs, cleaned
1 cup fresh buttered breadcrumbs

Melt butter in saucepan. Add flour and blend over low heat, stirring constantly, for 3 to 5 minutes. Slowly stir in milk. Cook and stir until thickened. Blend in mustard, salt and red pepper. Gently fold in crabmeat. • Prick legs and claws of each crab with the tines of a fork to prevent popping. Place crabs, bottom side up, on a broiling rack 3 inches from the heat. Brush with melted butter. Broil 4 to 5 minutes. Turn over, brush again with butter. Broil 4 to 5 minutes. • *To assemble:* Place about 3 tablespoons of the crab mixture on top of each broiled crab. Sprinkle with buttered crumbs. At serving time, bake in a preheated 350 degree oven for 15 minutes. *Serves 6.*

Total calories per serving: 309 • Percentage of calories from protein: 47 • Percentage of calories from carbohydrates: 4 • Percentage of calories from fat: 48 • Percentage of calories from saturated fat: 24

Boiled Spiced Crabs

Chef John Lockhart, Sr., Lockhart's Seafood Restaurant, Norfolk

12-16 live hard blue crabs
2-3 tablespoons pickling spice

In saucepan, bring water to a boil; add pickling spice (same spice used for pickles) and boil for 5 minutes. Add washed crabs and continue to boil for 35 minutes until pink. Serve with lemon wedges. *Serves 2.*

Crab, Orange And Avocado Salad

Chef Chris Goodwin, The Kitchen at Powhatan Plantation, Williamsburg

1 pound lump crabmeat, picked
2 oranges cut into sections
¼ cup mayonnaise or plain yogurt
pinch of Old Bay or other seafood seasoning
1 tablespoon fresh parsley
dash of fresh lemon juice
2 avocados, halved, seeded, peeled and sliced

Combine crabmeat, mayonnaise or yogurt, seafood seasoning, parsley and lemon juice. • *To assemble:* Place ½ sliced avocado in center of each plate. Place ¼ crabmeat mixture on top of avocado and top with ¼ of orange sections. *Serves 4.*

With yogurt
Total calories per serving: 665 • Percentage of calories from protein: 59 • Percentage of calories from carbohydrates: 7 • Percentage of calories from fat: 32 • Percentage of calories from saturated fat: 4

The soft-shell season is traditionally marked with the first full moon in May. At that time, the blue crab begins its molting season to accommodate its summer growth. The actual shedding of the shell can take anywhere from 1 to 3 hours, after which it must be removed from water or the hardening process will continue, reducing the quality of the soft-shell crab. Blue crabs shed numerous times during a single growing season.

Photo: Taran Z

Chesapeake Bay Blue Crab Cakes
Chef Todd Jurich, Bistro!, Norfolk

2 pounds fresh Chesapeake all lump blue crab, picked	2 tablespoons fresh parsley, chopped
⅓ cup fresh made mayonnaise	2 tablespoons green onion, finely chopped
1½ tablespoons dijon mustard	1 teaspoon zest of fresh lemon
2-3 extra large eggs	1 pinch of cayenne pepper
2 tablespoons lemon juice, freshly squeezed	2 teaspoons prepared horseradish
1 teaspoon Old Bay or other seafood seasoning	salt and black pepper, to taste
½ cup fresh soft bread crumbs	flour
	clarified butter or peanut oil for sauté

Combine all ingredients except crabmeat. Taste and adjust seasoning. Gently fold into crabmeat. Portion into 3½-ounce cakes. Lightly flour, sauté in clarified butter or peanut oil. Serve immediately. *Serves 6. Pictured at left.*

With tartar sauce, 4 tablespoons per serving
Total calories per serving: 448 • Percentage of calories from protein: 27 • Percentage of calories from carbohydrates: 4
Percentage of calories from fat: 68 • Percentage of calories from saturated fat: 10

Tartar Sauce

1 cup mayonnaise, preferably homemade	juice of 1 lemon
3 tablespoons dijon mustard	Old Bay or other seafood seasoning
1 teaspoon Worcestershire sauce	2 tablespoons parsley, chopped
1 teaspoon Tabasco or other red pepper sauce	1 tablespoon gherkins, finely chopped
1 tablespoon capers, drained and rinsed	1 teaspoon dry mustard
¼ cup celery, finely diced	1 tablespoon prepared horseradish
¼ cup spring onions or scallions, finely diced	

Combine all ingredients and puree, or, if desired, leave chunky. *Makes 2 cups.*

Cocktail Sauce From Hell
Chef Todd Jurich, Bistro!, Norfolk

2 cloves fresh garlic, minced	1 teaspoon Worcestershire sauce
¾ cup prepared fancy ketchup	1 teaspoon Old Bay or other seafood seasoning
1 tablespoon prepared spicy horseradish	¾ cup fresh aioli*
2 shakes Tabasco	
juice of 1 lemon	

Mix together. Serve cold. *Makes 2 cups. Pictured at left.*

* garlic mayonnaise

Dill-Dijon Butter

1 teaspoon olive oil	¼ cup clam juice
½ teaspoon shallots, chopped	¼ cup white wine
½ teaspoon garlic, chopped	1 tablespoon butter
1 tablespoon Dijon mustard	1 tablespoon chopped fresh dill

Sauté shallots and garlic in olive oil until shallots are soft; add mustard, clam juice and wine. Reduce to half the volume, then swirl in butter and dill.

Translation of its Latin name is "beautiful swimmer," and indeed it is, for its legs allow it to rapidly outdistance its other bottom crawling crab relatives. The blue crab's common name is equally telling, recognizing the bright blue coloration of its claws. The female of the species is even more vivid, setting off her pincers with bright red tips.

Crab Cakes Lynnhaven Inlet
Chef Joseph Zaremski, Lynnhaven Fish House, Virginia Beach

- 1 pound backfin crabmeat
- 1 cup bread crumbs (unseasoned)
- 4 medium eggs
- 2 tablespoons prepared mustard
- 1 tablespoon vegetable oil
- 1 teaspoon sugar
- salt and pepper, to taste
- oil for deep frying
- parsley and lemon wedges for garnish

Mix all ingredients in order. Shape into 6 medium-thick discs. Heat oil to 350 degrees. Add crabcakes. Cook until golden brown. Serve hot with parsley and lemon wedges. *Serves 6.*

Total calories per serving: 352 • Percentage of calories from protein: 21 • Percentage of calories from carbohydrates: 4
Percentage of calories from fat: 73 • Percentage of calories from saturated fat: 11

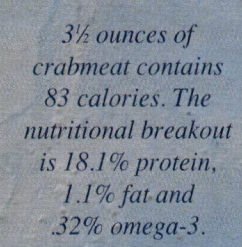

Eastern Shore Jumbo Crabmeat With Local Asparagus And Cilantro Mustard Sauce
Chef Amy E. Brandt, The Lucky Star, Virginia Beach

- 6 chilled salad plates
- 1 pound jumbo lump crabmeat
- 1½ pounds fresh asparagus
- ice
- lemon juice, to taste
- salt and pepper, to taste

Dump crabmeat onto cookie sheet; carefully pick through the crabmeat for remaining shell particles. Be very careful not to crush the lumps during this process or you will ruin the product's appearance. Refrigerate immediately. • In a large bowl, place ice and water. Set aside. • Wash and trim asparagus. Fill a pot, large enough to accommodate the asparagus, ¾ full of water seasoned with salt and lemon juice. Bring water to boil and immerse asparagus; simmer until asparagus has cooked but is crispy. Cooking time will vary due to thickness of stems. Carefully remove from the pot and place in the ice and water bath. Let set in water until fully cooled. Drain and place on paper towel lined tray; refrigerate. • *To assemble:* Place asparagus on the chilled plates; arrange in a fan with the stems together and the tips apart. Place approximately 3 ounces of crabmeat near the bottom of the stems. Drizzle 2 ounces of the cilantro mustard sauce over both the crabmeat and the asparagus. Serve immediately or assemble without the dressing and refrigerate. *Serves 6.*

Cilantro Mustard Sauce

- 4 tablespoons Dijon mustard
- 2 cups olive oil
- ¼ cup lime juice
- 1 tablespoon raspberry vinegar
- 2 tablespoons cilantro leaves, carefully chopped
- 3 tablespoons tomato, diced and seeded
- salt and pepper, to taste

Place the mustard in a medium bowl. Whisk in the olive oil in a slow steady stream. Whisk in the lime juice, diced tomato, raspberry vinegar and cilantro. Season to taste with salt and pepper.

Total calories per serving: 462
Percentage of calories from protein: 17
Percentage of calories from carbohydrates: 7
Percentage of calories from fat: 75
Percentage of calories from saturated fat: 10

3½ ounces of crabmeat contains 83 calories. The nutritional breakout is 18.1% protein, 1.1% fat and .32% omega-3.

Virginia Ham And Blue Crab Chowder
Chef J. David Everett, C.E.C., the Dining Room At Ford's Colony, Williamsburg

4 ounces smoked bacon, diced	sea salt
1 large onion, diced	pepper, freshly ground
2 cloves garlic, minced	1 bay leaf
3 stalks celery, diced	½ quart crab stock
1 large potato, diced	1 quart heavy cream or half & half
¼ cup Virginia ham, diced	2 ounces dry sherry
8 ounces crab meat, picked	

Place smoked bacon in soup pot and begin to sauté. When the fat has been released from the bacon, add the onion, garlic and celery, and sauté. • Add potatoes and continue cooking. Add the Virginia ham, followed by the spices and season to taste. • Add crab stock and heavy cream, bring to a boil, reduce heat and simmer for 20 to 30 minutes or until thick enough to coat the back of a spoon. • Adjust seasoning and add sherry. Serve with additional cooked potatoes, lump crab meat and chopped chives. *Serves 4 to 6.*

Based upon 6 servings
Total calories per serving: 447 • Percentage of calories from protein: 22 • Percentage of calories from carbohydrates: 14
Percentage of calories from fat: 61 • Percentage of calories from saturated fat: 31

Tomato Angel Hair Pasta With Tomato Concasse, Butter, Fresh Basil, Garlic And Jumbo Lump Crabmeat
Chef Monroe Duncan, Monroe's, Norfolk

8 ounces fresh jumbo lump crabmeat	1 teaspoon fresh garlic, minced
6 ounces whole butter, lightly salted or unsalted	2 teaspoons fresh parsley, chopped
1 fresh tomato, finely chopped	8 ounces fresh tomato angel hair pasta, uncooked
8 large fresh basil leaves	

Important to the success of this dish is the use of very fresh ingredients. This dish must be served as soon as it has been prepared. It doesn't wait! • Keep a boiling pot of water with strainer ready as you begin the sauce preparation. • Add butter to sauté pan with garlic and basil leaves. Slightly brown the garlic as the basil leaves wilt. Add the tomato concasse (with natural juice) and bring to a boil. At this point, place the tomato angel hair in strainer, then into the boiling water. • Add chopped parsley and crabmeat to the tomato concasse mixture. Heat the crabmeat thoroughly in the sauce, but do not shred the lumps of the crabmeat with overmixing. • Fresh tomato angel hair pasta will require 90 seconds in the boiling water to cook. Remove and shake excess water from pasta. • *To assemble:* Place pasta in bowl and pour sauce with crabmeat over the pasta. Garnish with fresh sprig of basil and serve at once. *Serves 2 to 3.*

Based upon 2 servings
Total calories per serving: 852 • Percentage of calories from protein: 12 • Percentage of calories from carbohydrates: 12
Percentage of calories from fat: 74 • Percentage of calories from saturated fat: 45

Select crabmeat to suit your recipes. "Backfin" or "lump backfin" consists of solid lumps of white meat and is perfect for recipes where appearance is important. "Flake" (either regular or special) consists of small pieces of white meat from the body of the crab. "Claw meat" as its name indicates comes from the appendages. It has a slightly brownish color.

Virginia is the third largest seafood producing state.

Smithfield Backfin Crab Rollup With James River Sauce

2 teaspoons Dijon mustard
½ teaspoon Old Bay or other seafood seasoning
1 teaspoon paprika
2 eggs, beaten
½ cup breadcrumbs
1 pound backfin crabmeat, loosely picked to remove shells
½ pound Smithfield ham, thinly sliced

Blend mustard, seasonings, and eggs together. • Fold in breadcrumbs and crabmeat. • Form into cylinders 5 inches long, ½ inch wide. • Place on cookie sheet and chill. Bake at 325 degrees, until firm, about 20 minutes. • Wrap ham around crabmeat cylinders and fasten with tooth picks every ½ inch. Cut between tooth picks and serve with James River Sauce. *Serves 6.*

James River Sauce

¼ cup white wine
¼ cup sour cream
1 tablespoon Old Bay or other seafood seasoning
1 lemon (use the juice from lemon and ¼ teaspoon lemon zest)*

Blend all ingredients in blender and serve cold as dip for rollups.

* *The zest is the colored part of the citrus peel with none of the bitter white membrane.*

Total calories per serving: 227
Percentage of calories from protein: 47
Percentage of calories from carbohydrates: 6
Percentage of calories from fat: 40
Percentage of calories from saturated fat: 16

Virginia Waterfront Blue Crab Feast

Serve crabs heaped on table covered with newspaper.

½ cup Old Bay or other seafood seasoning
½ teaspoon cayenne pepper or red pepper flakes *(optional)*
2 tablespoons salt
2 cups white vinegar
2 cups beer *or* water
24 live blue crabs

In a large steamer or pot with a raised rack and tight-fitting lid, combine vinegar, water or beer and bring to a boil. Combine spices and blend well. Place one-half of the crabs in the pot. Sprinkle one half of the spice mixture over the crabs. Add remaining crabs. Sprinkle remaining spice mixture over them. Cover. Steam about 25 to 35 minutes. Crabs will turn bright red. To serve, spread a thick layer of newspaper on the table. Provide wooden mallets, a paring knife and paper towels. Heap steamed crabs in the center of the table. *Serves 4.*

Total calories per serving: 172 • Percentage of calories from protein: 83 • Percentage of calories from carbohydrates: 0 • Percentage of calories from fat: 16 • Percentage of calories from saturated fat: 2

Norfolk Crabmeat In Butter

Chef John Lockhart, Sr., Lockhart's Seafood Restaurant, Norfolk

5-6 ounces backfin lump crabmeat, picked
butter, melted
1 dash of hot sauce *or* lemon juice
fresh mushrooms *(optional)*

Place crabmeat in casserole baking dish and coat top of crabmeat with melted butter. Add a dash of hot sauce or lemon juice. Brown top lightly and serve hot. For an added treat, include fresh mushrooms. *Serves 1.*

Total calories per serving: 296 • Percentage of calories from protein: 39 • Percentage of calories from carbohydrates: 0 • Percentage of calories from fat: 60 • Percentage of calories from saturated fat: 33

Pirates Style Fish Stew

Chef Chris Goodwin, The Kitchen At Powhatan Plantation, Williamsburg

2½ pounds clean Virginia waterfront fillets of assorted fish (sea bass, sea trout, mackerel, etc.)
¼ cup olive oil
4 ounces celery, diced
4 ounces onion, diced
4 ounces fennel, diced
4 ounces carrot, diced
1 cup tomato concasse with juice
8 small red bliss potatoes, diced
1 cup peas or green beans
1 clove garlic, minced
1 tablespoon thyme, finely chopped
1 tablespoon oregano, finely chopped
1 tablespoon fresh parsley, finely chopped
1 bottle dry white wine
½ gallon fish stock
1 pinch saffron
1 teaspoon lemon juice
1½ teaspoons hot cayenne pepper
salt and pepper, to taste

Cut fish fillets into 2-ounce pieces (approximately 40). In a heavy-bottomed stock pot, heat oil until hot. Sweat vegetables until just soft. Add tomato concasse with juice; cook 3 to 4 minutes. Add garlic. Season lightly with salt and pepper. Add wine and bring to a boil. Add fish stock and bring to a boil. Add potatoes and green peas or beans. Add spices. Cook until vegetables are al dente. Add fish and cook 5 minutes. Finish with lemon juice and salt and pepper to taste. Ladle into large bowls and serve with toasted cornbread. *Serving size: approximately 12 to 15 large bowls.*

Based upon 12 large bowls
Total calories per serving: 332 • Percentage of calories from protein: 33 • Percentage of calories from carbohydrates: 19 Percentage of calories from fat: 32 • Percentage of calories from saturated fat: 5

A fillet is a boneless piece of fish that has been cut away from the backbone.

A fish steak is a crosscut slice from a large, dressed fish.

Crispy Fried Shad Roe With Mirepoix Of Tomato, Onion, Provence Olives And Lemon Zest

Chef J. David Everett, C.E.C., The Dining Room At Ford's Colony, Williamsburg

1 cup beer or ale
1 cup flour
1 tablespoon cornstarch
1 teaspoon white sugar
  sea salt, to taste
  ground black pepper, to taste
  cayenne pepper, to taste
2 ice cubes
4 shad roe sacks (2 pairs or sets)
  oil for frying

Mirepoix

3 ounces olive oil
½ cup onion, diced
½ cup tomato concasse (small diced tomato)
¼ cup Provence olives
4 anchovy fillets, diced
2 tablespoons lemon zest*
3 ounces balsamic vinegar
  black pepper, to taste
⅛ cup fresh basil, julienned

Combine beer, flour, cornstarch, sugar, sea salt, black pepper and cayenne pepper. Mix well. Refrigerate until use. • At the time of frying, add 2 ice cubes to the batter. • Dip and fry shad roe in about ½ inch of oil, until golden brown.

Total calories per serving: 265
Percentage of calories from protein: 14
Percentage of calories from carbohydrates: 4
Percentage of calories from fat: 79
Percentage of calories from saturated fat: 11

Sauté the onion in olive oil. Add tomato concasse, olives, anchovies, lemon zest, balsamic vinegar, black pepper and mix well. • *To assemble:* Place mixture in center of plate; place shad on top, followed by fresh basil. *Serves 4.*

* *The zest is the colored part of the citrus peel with none of the bitter white membrane.*

Pepper Seared Yellow Fin Tuna Filled With Virginia Goats' Cheese, Sundried Tomatoes, Shiitake Mushrooms, Fresh Basil And Garlic

Chef Amy Brandt, The Lucky Star, Virginia Beach

- 4 tuna steaks (8 ounces each *or* 1" each), butterflied
- 4 ounces Virginia goats' cheese
- 1 ounce sundried tomatoes
- 8 shiitake mushrooms, stems removed
- 8 large basil leaves
- 2 cloves garlic, finely chopped and mixed with 3 tablespoons olive oil
- 1½ ounces olive oil

In a hot sauté pan, heat ½ ounce olive oil. Place the mushroom caps top side down in the hot pan. Sear until slightly crisp, turn and sear briefly. Remove from heat and set aside. • Preheat oven to 400 degrees. • *To assemble:* Open butterflied tuna, place on the bottom flap in this order: 1 ounce goats' cheese, ¼ ounce sundried tomato strips, 2 large shiitake mushrooms and 2 basil leaves. Brush the inside of the top flap with the garlic oil. Close and grind black pepper on both sides. Set aside. • Heat a heavy gauge, oven proof sauté pan (example: cast iron) large enough to hold the four filled tuna steaks. When hot, add 1 ounce olive oil. Carefully place the stuffed tuna in the pan. Sear until brown. Turning over may be tricky. Try picking up the tuna with a spatula and put your hand on the top uncooked side and invert on a counter top. Slide spatula under the tuna and replace in the pan. Place in oven; bake 5 to 10 minutes or until done. Place on hot plates or platter and keep warm. Serves 4. *Pictured at right.*

Total calories per serving: 552 • Percentage of calories from protein: 40 • Percentage of calories from carbohydrates: 2 • Percentage of calories from fat: 56 • Percentage of calories from saturated fat: 13

Pan Seared Tuna With Curry Dipping Sauce

Proprietor Peter Coe and Chef Dina Walker, Taste Unlimited, Virginia Beach and Norfolk

- 1 pound fresh tuna
- 1 cup flour
- 2 teaspoons salt
- 1 teaspoon white pepper
- vegetable oil for searing

Curry Dipping Sauce

- ¼ cup Major Grey chutney
- ½ cup mayonnaise
- ½ cup plain yogurt
- 1 teaspoon curry powder
- ½ teaspoon Dijon mustard

Trim tuna, removing any dark red portions. Cut into bite-sized cubes. • Combine flour, salt and pepper. Lightly coat tuna with the seasoned flour, shaking off any excess (a mesh strainer works well). • Place 2 tablespoons of oil in a very hot sauté pan. Sear tuna (about 6 pieces at a time depending on the size of the pan) very quickly, making sure that all sides are brown. Be sure not to overcook or overcrowd. Tuna is best left a little pink inside. Place each piece of tuna on a 6-inch skewer and serve warm with the curry dipping sauce. *One pound of tuna yields 30 to 40 pieces.*

Puree chutney in a food processor. Mix with remaining ingredients. Color will intensify after several hours. Refrigerate until ready to use.

Based upon 5 servings of 8 one-inch tuna pieces
Total calories per serving: 313
Percentage of calories from protein: 36
Percentage of calories from carbohydrates: 8
Percentage of calories from fat: 54
Percentage of calories from saturated fat: 8

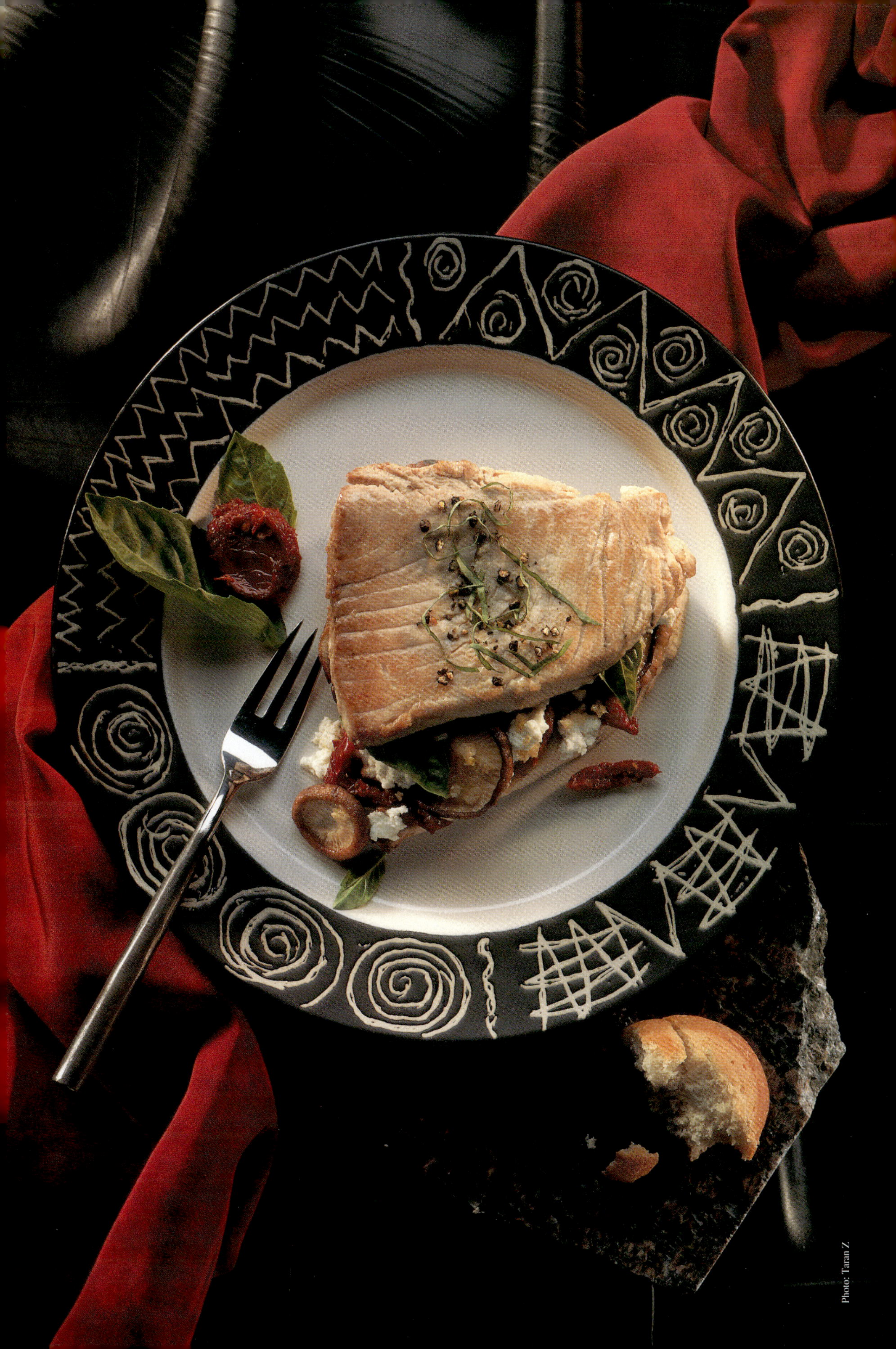

Photo: Taran Z

Sautéed Fresh Tuna Medallion Oriental

Chef Tom Evaldi C.E.C., Gus' Mariner Restaurant, Virginia Beach

- 4 fresh tuna steaks (6 ounces each)
- 1 cup teriyaki sauce
- 1 cup blush wine
- ½ bunch green onions, chopped
- 2 tablespoons sugar
- 2 tablespoons sesame oil
- 4 ounces snow peas, julienned
- 4 ounces red peppers, julienned
- 4 ounces carrots, julienned
- chopped garlic, to taste
- sesame oil for sautéeing

Combine teriyaki sauce, wine, green onion, sugar and sesame oil for marinade. Place the tuna steaks in marinade for approximately 2 hours. • After 2 hours, pat the tuna steaks dry and sauté until browned on the outside and still moist and pink in the center. Hold in warm place. • Sauté the vegetables and garlic in sesame oil, over high heat, and finish with a little of the marinade. Keep the vegetables crisp. • Arrange the nest of vegetables around the tuna steak. *Serves 4.*

Total calories per serving: 321 • Percentage of calories from protein: 66 • Percentage of calories from carbohydrates: 9
Percentage of calories from fat: 23 • Percentage of calories from saturated fat: 3

Rockfish On Bed Of Leeks

Proprietor Joe Hoggard and Chef Bobby Huber, Jr., The Ships Cabin, Norfolk

- 4 rockfish fillets (6 ounces each)
- 8 ounces capers
- juice of 1 lemon
- 2 ounces dry white wine
- 4 ounces fish stock
- 4 tablespoons butter, melted
- 3 leeks
- 2 tablespoons sugar
- salt and pepper, to taste

Place rockfish fillets in baking dish. Pour wine, capers, fish stock, butter and half of the lemon juice over fish. Salt and pepper to taste. Place in 400 degree oven approximately 8 to 12 minutes, basting periodically. • Cut leeks lengthwise and wash thoroughly. Slice in julienne strips. Sauté in butter until tender. Stir in remaining lemon juice, sugar, salt and pepper. • *To assemble:* Serve fillets over bed of leeks. Top with remaining sauce from baking pan. Garnish with parsley and lemon. *Serves 4.*

Total calories per serving: 332 • Percentage of calories from protein: 35 • Percentage of calories from carbohydrates: 13
Percentage of calories from fat: 48 • Percentage of calories from saturated fat: 22

Horseradish-Crusted Rockfish

Chef Michael Toepper, Fire & Ice Restaurant, Hampton

- 4 rockfish fillets (6 ounces each)
- ⅓ cup mayonnaise
- 2 tablespoons horseradish
- 1 tablespoon bread crumbs
- ½ teaspoon minced garlic
- 1 anchovy fillet *(optional)*
- 1 pinch white pepper
- flour to coat

Blend mayonnaise, horseradish, bread crumbs, garlic, anchovy and pepper in food processor. Dredge rockfish in flour then coat with horseradish mixture. Bake in 350 degree oven for 9 to 12 minutes until fish flakes easily with a fork. • Serve with Dill-Dijon Butter (recipe on page 15). *Serves 4.*

Total calories per serving: 390 • Percentage of calories from protein: 39 • Percentage of calories from carbohydrates: 3
Percentage of calories from fat: 55 • Percentage of calories from saturated fat: 13

Barbecued Bluefish*

4 whole Virginia bluefish, pan dressed *or*
   2 pounds bluefish fillets or steaks
1½ cups Hot and Spicy Basting Sauce
   parsley
   lemon wedges

Hot And Spicy Basting Sauce

½ cup honey
½ cup prepared mustard
½ cup cider vinegar
¼ cup Worcestershire sauce
1 tablespoon parsley flakes
1-2 teaspoons liquid hot pepper sauce
1 teaspoon salt
1 teaspoon cornstarch or arrowroot

Wash and dry fish. Grease a hinged-wire hand grill and place fish between the two racks. If a hand grill is not available, grease your grill rack and use a metal spatula for turning. Brush both sides of the fish with Hot and Spicy Basting Sauce and position the hand grill on grill rack 4 to 6 inches from moderately hot coals. Cook 8 minutes, baste and turn fish. Cook an additional 8 to 10 minutes or until flesh flakes easily when tested with a fork. Allow 16 to 20 minutes total cooking time. Garnish barbecued bluefish with parsley and lemon wedges. *Serves 4.*

Blend honey and mustard in a saucepan on the grill. Stir in vinegar, Worcestershire sauce, parsley flakes, hot pepper sauce and salt. Add cornstarch or arrowroot and cook, stirring over coals until mixture comes to a boil and thickens. *Makes about 1½ cups.*

* *Sea trout may be substituted for bluefish.*

Total calories per serving: 284• Percentage of calories from protein: 51• Percentage of calories from carbohydrates: 26 Percentage of calories from fat: 22 • Percentage of calories from saturated fat: 4

Smokey Marinated Mackerel*

8 Virginia Atlantic or Spanish Mackerel steaks
   or fillets
1½ cups Lemon-Wine Marinade

Lemon-Wine Marinade

1 cup butter or margarine
½ cup dry white wine
1½ tablespoons fresh-squeezed or bottled
   lemon juice
½ teaspoon pepper
½ teaspoon salt
¼ teaspoon tarragon
¼ teaspoon rosemary

Wash and dry fish, and stack them in a large mixing bowl. Pour Lemon-Wine Marinade over fish and let stand in a covered bowl for 30 minutes, turning once. Place marinated fish on the grill rack at least 6 inches from smoking coals for slow cooking, which will keep the fish moist and make it easy to remove. Close down the grill lid, or cover rack with a piece of foil and "smoke" fish. After 30 minutes, carefully lift the cover or foil and turn each fish with a spatula. Baste fish with the remaining marinade. Replace cover and cook 20 to 25 more minutes. Serve hot off the grill. *Serves 4.*

Melt butter in a saucepan on the grill. Add wine, lemon and seasonings. Cook until mixture is warm. Do not boil. *Makes about 1½ cups.*

Total calories per serving: 453
Percentage of calories from protein: 30
Percentage of calories from carbohydrates: 0
Percentage of calories from fat: 67
Percentage of calories from saturated fat: 32

* *Tuna, Bluefish, Catfish or Drum may be substituted for Mackerel.*

Optional variation: For a wood-smoked flavor, soak one pound of hickory chips in a bucket of water for two hours. Cover glowing charcoal briquettes with damp hickory chips to produce smoke and lower the temperature for slow cooking.

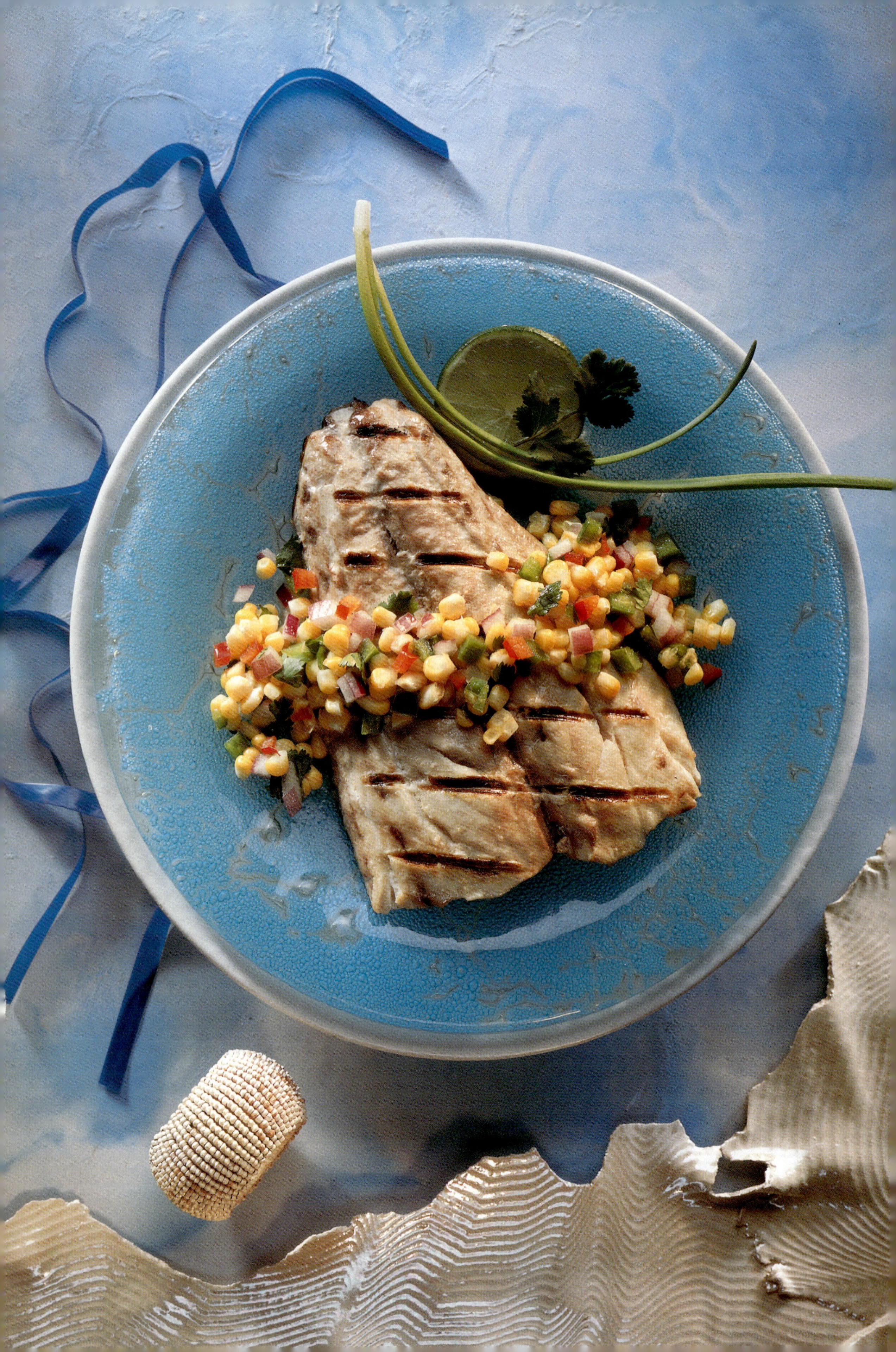

Grilled Taylor Blues With Fresh Corn Salsa
Chef Chris Goodwin, The Kitchen at Powhatan Plantation, Williamsburg

- 4 bluefish fillets (6 - 8 ounces each)
- 3 ears fresh or frozen corn, kernels removed
- 6 sprigs fresh cilantro, roughly chopped
- 2 teaspoons red onion, finely diced
- 1 teaspoon green pepper, finely diced
- 1 jalapeno, seeded and finely chopped
- 2 limes, juice removed and saved
- 1 pinch cumin
-   salt, to taste
-   cracked black pepper, to taste
- 1 teaspoon canola oil

To make salsa: mix all vegetables and spices together in a non-corrosive bowl. Toss; cover for at least one hour. • Brush filets with oil. On a medium-hot, clean grill, cook bluefish fillets for 2 to 3 minutes on each side. Remove from grill and place in 225 degree oven for 3 to 5 minutes. • While fillets are in the oven, heat skillet until it is hot, add salsa and cook approximately 2 minutes or until all ingredients are warm. Remove from heat. • *To assemble:* Arrange Bluefish on plates and garnish with salsa. *Serves 4. Pictured at left.*

Total calories per serving: 520 • Percentage of calories from protein: 29 • Percentage of calories from carbohydrates: 49 Percentage of calories from fat: 20 • Percentage of calories from saturated fat: 4

Cedar Planked Sea Trout On Fresh Shiitake Mushrooms With Tomato-Basil Compote
Chef J. David Everett, C.E.C., The Dining Room At Ford's Colony, Williamsburg

- 4 sea trout fillets (8 ounces each)
- 2 ounces olive oil
-   sea salt, to taste
-   pepper, freshly ground, to taste
- 2 cedar planks
-   Shiitake Mushroom Sauté
-   Tomato-Basil Compote

Brush the fillets and planks with olive oil. • Season the fillets. • Place skin side up on cedar plank or in a baking dish and bake in 350 degree oven for 3 to 6 minutes. Flip and continue to cook until slightly firm to the touch. • Place on Shiitake mushrooms and top with 1 tablespoon of Tomato-Basil Compote.

Shiitake Mushroom Sauté

- 2 ounces olive oil
- 1 shallot
- 3 cloves garlic
-   sea salt, to taste
-   pepper, freshly ground, to taste
- 4 cups Shiitake mushrooms, sliced
- 3 ounces white wine
- 1 tablespoon parsley, chopped

Sauté the shallots and garlic in olive oil until translucent. Season to taste. • Add the mushrooms and sauté until soft. Deglaze with wine. Drain excess liquid, add parsley and place in center of the plate.

Total calories per serving: 876
Percentage of calories from protein: 20
Percentage of calories from carbohydrates: 8
Percentage of calories from fat: 69
Percentage of calories from saturated fat: 10

Tomato-Basil Compote

- 2 ounces olive oil
- ½ onion, diced
- 4 cloves garlic, minced
-   sea salt, to taste
-   pepper, freshly ground, to taste
- ½ tablespoon fresh basil, chopped
- 6 ounces olive oil
- 2 tablespoons Balsamic vinegar
- 2 fresh tomatoes, finely diced
- 1½ cups canned tomatoes, diced
- 1 tablespoon tomato paste

Sauté the onion and garlic in olive oil until translucent. Season with sea salt and pepper then cool completely. Combine the remaining ingredients and add to the above. Refrigerate overnight. Mix well and serve on Cedar Planked Trout. *Serves 4.*

Here's an easy rule to remember. Almost any fish, either whole or fillet, can be baked to perfection by cooking 10 minutes for each inch of thickness at about 425 to 450 degrees.

Potato Chip Encrusted Striped Bass With Sautéed Backfin Crab, Papaya And Fresh Pineapple

Chef Chuck Sass, Mahi Mah's Seafood Restaurant and Sushi Saloon, Virginia Beach

4 skinless striped bass fillets (6 ounces each)
1 ounce flour
3 ounces buttermilk
2 cups salted plain potato chips, crushed
4 ounces. clarified butter
½ pound fresh backfin crabmeat
½ cup fresh pineapple, diced
2 tablespoons fresh shallots, chopped
½ cup fresh papaya, diced
1 ounce fresh orange juice
1 ounce dry white wine
2 tablespoons fresh cilantro
3 tablespoons whole butter, soft
salt, to taste
white pepper, to taste

Dredge the striped bass fillets in flour, then buttermilk, and finally crushed potato chips. • In large skillet, heat the clarified butter and brown the fillets on both sides, being careful not to burn the potato chips. When brown, place on baking pan and place in 350 degree oven for approximately 5 minutes or until fillets are cooked. • Pour off excess grease from the skillet and add shallots, papayas, and pineapples. Cook for one minute on medium heat, and deglaze pan with the white wine and the orange juice. Add fresh cilantro and gently fold the crab and the whole butter into the sauce. Season with salt and pepper. • Remove the fillets from the oven and pour the sauce over the fish. *Serves 4. Pictured at right.*

Total calories per serving: 432 • Percentage of calories from protein: 37 • Percentage of calories from carbohydrates: 13
Percentage of calories from fat: 47 • Percentage of calories from saturated fat: 19

Sea Trout Norfolk

Charlie Sears, The Max, Portsmouth

4 fresh, whole grey sea trout (1¼ pounds each), heads on, cleaned and gutted
seafood seasoning
3 large lemons
1 medium onion
1 stalk celery, cut into four 2-inch pieces
12 jumbo shrimp, raw and headless
½ cup white wine
vegetable oil for coating
⅓ cup butter, melted
1 cup wild rice, uncooked
4 whole cherries
4 sprigs endive, for garnish

Starting 3 inches behind the gills, vertically cut the fish to the bones in 3 places, about 1½ inches apart. Make cuts 2½ inches long. Rub seafood seasoning over the entire fish. • Cut 24 paper-thin slices of lemon, plus 8 equal wedges. Slice the onion into 4 equal wedges. Stuff the cavity of each fish with a wedge of lemon, onion, and a piece of celery. Place 2 lemon slices in each vertical cut, forming a V-shaped cradle for the shrimp (to be added later). • Cover the fish tail with aluminum foil (to prevent burning). Put the fish in a covered container and refrigerate 1 hour. • Preheat the oven to 375 degrees. • Place the fish in a baking dish lightly coated with vegetable oil. Pour the melted butter over the fish and cook approximately 35 minutes, testing with a fork until it penetrates easily. • Meanwhile, prepare the wild rice according to package directions. • When the fish has about 5 minutes left to cook, remove it from the oven. Place 1 shrimp in each lemon cradle and fan the shrimp tails. Pour the wine over the fish and return to the oven for 5 minutes. • Serve over a bed of wild rice. Skewer the remaining lemon wedges, cherries and endive on toothpicks for garnish. If desired, the trout may be accompanied by dill or tartar sauce. *Serves 4.*

Total calories per serving: 574 • Percentage of calories from protein: 33 • Percentage of calories from carbohydrates: 12
Percentage of calories from fat: 50 • Percentage of calories from saturated fat: 19

Here are some guidelines for purchasing fish. For each serving, you will need: 12 ounces of whole fish; 8 ounces drawn or dressed fish and 4 to 6 ounces steaks or fillets.

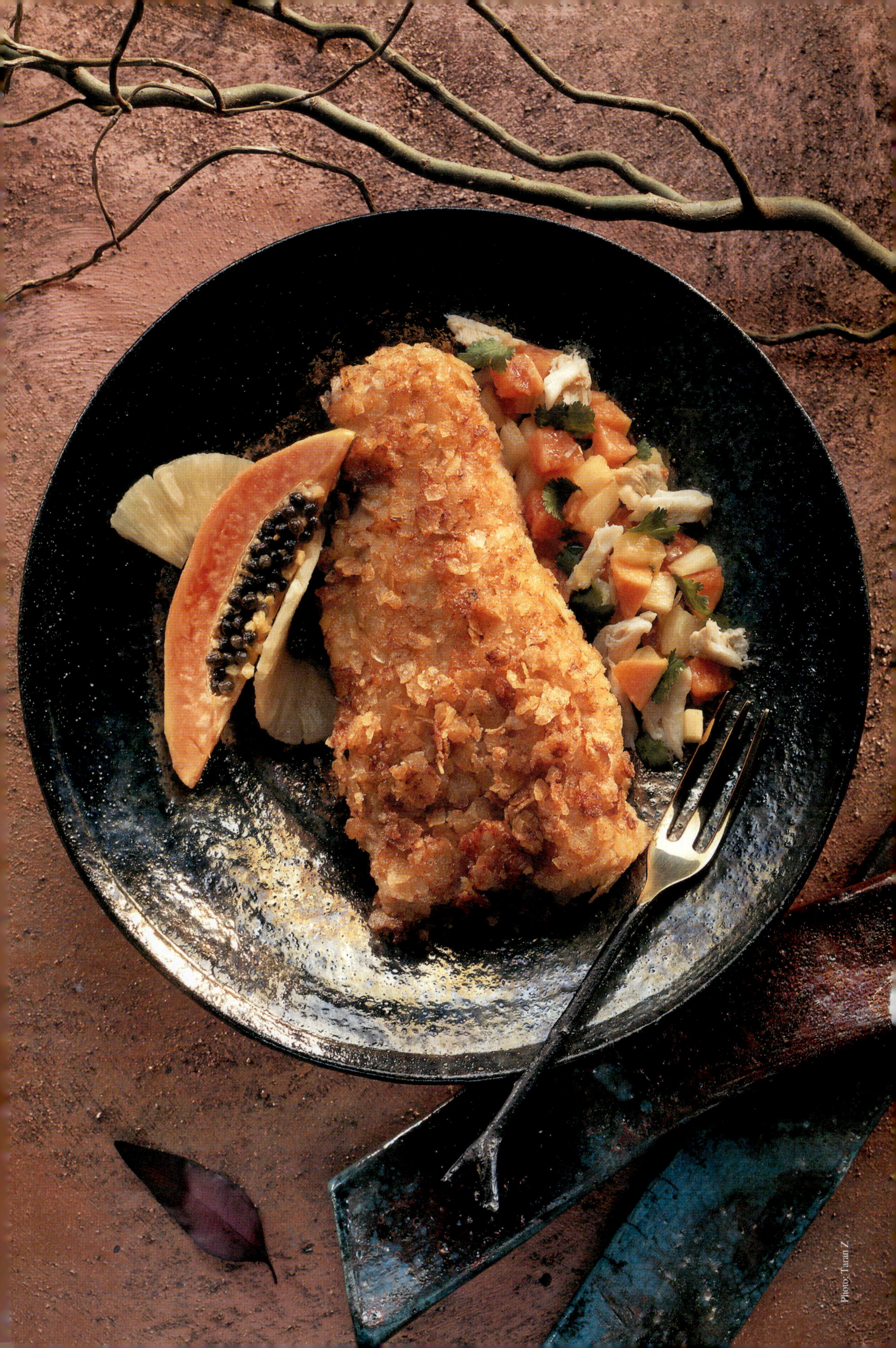
Photo: Taran Z

Steamed Black Sea Bass

1 sea bass (1-1½ pounds), cleaned, whole with head on
4 slices ginger root, shredded
2 tablespoons black beans
1 teaspoon sherry
2 garlic cloves, smashed
¼ cup peanut oil
1 handful green onions, chopped
½ cup liquid for steaming (wine, fish stock, water, etc.)

Make 4 slashes in the flesh of the fish with a knife, cutting to the bone. • Mix the ginger slices, black beans and sherry together in a small bowl, mashing the beans lightly with a spoon. • Fill the cavities of the fish (they won't be filled by this amount, so really "place" some in the cavities), and on both sides of the exterior. • Place fish on aluminum foil or on a platter and steam about 20 minutes. • Remove from steamer, keep warm and quickly brown the garlic in oil. Pour the flavored oil over the fish, sprinkle with garnish and serve. *Serves 2.*

Total calories per serving: 441 • Percentage of calories from protein: 36 • Percentage of calories from carbohydrates: 6
Percentage of calories from fat: 57 • Percentage of calories from saturated fat: 9

Mahi Mahi With Christo Sauce

Chef Tom Evaldi, C.E.C., Gus' Mariner Restaurant, Virginia Beach

4 fillets of fresh mahi mahi (8-10 ounces each)
melted butter for basting
Old Bay or other seafood seasoning
1 lemon
4 ounces butter
2 teaspoons garlic, minced
2 fresh tomatoes, diced
1 can (14 ounces) artichoke hearts, quartered
8 ounces fresh mushrooms, sliced
4 tablespoons capers
2 tablespoons fresh parsley, chopped
8 ounces dry white wine

Place the mahi mahi fillets on a sheet pan; baste with butter. Squeeze the fresh lemon over the filets and sprinkle lightly with seafood seasoning. • Place the fillets in a 450 degree oven and bake until firm to the touch (10 to 15 minutes). Spoon the Christo Sauce over the baked mahi mahi and serve immediately. *Serves 4.*

Christo Sauce

Place a sauté pan on the stove over high heat. Add 4 ounces of butter and melt. Add the garlic and sauté until it becomes tan in color. Add the tomatoes, artichoke hearts, mushrooms, capers and chopped parsley; sauté until all vegetables are heated thoroughly. Add the white wine to the pan, allowing it to reduce until the sauce has a slightly thickened appearance.

Total calories per serving: 497
Percentage of calories from protein: 42
Percentage of calories from carbohydrates: 5
Percentage of calories from fat: 44
Percentage of calories from saturated fat: 26

Flounder Baked In Parchment With Tomatoes, Red Onion, Garlic, Lemon Zest And Rosemary

Chef Amy E. Brandt, The Lucky Star, Virginia Beach

- 4 (6-8 ounces each) fresh skinless flounder fillets
- 1 medium red onion, sliced
- 8 roma tomatoes, diced and seeded
- 3 cloves garlic, peeled and thinly sliced
- zest and juice of 1 lemon
- 2 teaspoons fresh rosemary, chopped
- 1 teaspoon fresh oregano
- 2 teaspoons fresh basil
- 4 tablespoons parsley, roughly chopped
- ½ teaspoon ground black pepper
- 1 teaspoon balsamic vinegar
- sea salt to taste
- 4 pieces of parchment paper (16"x24" each)
- olive oil

Peel and julienne the red onion and set aside. Toss together in a large bowl: roma tomatoes, garlic, chopped lemon zest and juice, rosemary, oregano, basil, parsley, balsamic vinegar, pepper and sea salt. • *To assemble:* Fold the parchment in half and cut out a heart as you would a valentine. Open the heart with the point facing you and lightly brush the middle of the right side with olive oil. Place one of the flounder filets on the oiled area. Place some red onions then some of the tomato mixture on the flounder fillet. Close the heart and fold in the edges starting at the rounded side. Be sure to crease tightly for a good seal. Repeat with remaining portions. • Place packages on cookie sheet and bake in a preheated 400 degree oven for 10 minutes. *Serves 4. Fish can be served in its package or removed to a plate. I suggest serving Orzo pasta with the dish.*

Total calories per serving: 227 • Percentage of calories from protein: 63 • Percentage of calories from carbohydrates: 8
Percentage of calories from fat: 27 • Percentage of calories from saturated fat: 5

Ocean View Flounder

Proprietor Joe Hoggard and Chef Bobby Huber Jr., The Ships Cabin, Norfolk

- 4 flounder fillets (6 ounces each)
- 4 tablespoons all-purpose flour
- ½ teaspoon salt
- fresh ground pepper, to taste
- 2 teaspoons extra-virgin olive oil
- 4 cloves garlic
- 2 tablespoons parsley, chopped
- ¼ teaspoon crushed red pepper flakes
- 1 can (28 ounces) plum tomatoes, drained and coarsely chopped
- ½ cup fish stock or clam juice

Lightly dust flounder with flour and season with salt and pepper. Set aside. • Heat olive oil in 10-inch skillet over medium heat. Add garlic, parsley, and pepper flakes and sauté for 30 seconds; do not let garlic brown. • Add tomatoes and fish stock. • Place flounder in pan and spoon sauce over it so the fish is covered. Adjust heat so sauce is at a very slow simmer. Cook until flounder is just cooked through, about 15 minutes. Remove from heat and seal skillet with aluminum foil. Set aside until ready to serve; the dish should be served warm but not hot. Carefully lift fillets out of skillet with a spatula, place on plates and spoon sauce over top. *Serves 4.*

Total calories per serving: 295 • Percentage of calories from protein: 38 • Percentage of calories from carbohydrates: 26
Percentage of calories from fat: 34 • Percentage of calories from saturated fat: 6

The old adage "flat as a flounder" should more properly be "flat as a mature flounder", because these "flatfish", as they are called, are born swimming in vertical position, but undergo a bizarre metamorphosis as they mature. One eye moves across the top of the head until it rests close beside the other; the head becomes twisted and the mouth is adjusted toward one side. It also adjusts its color to blend with its environment, thereby preparing for its life lying on or swimming near the bottom.

Seasonal Availability Of Fresh Virginia Species

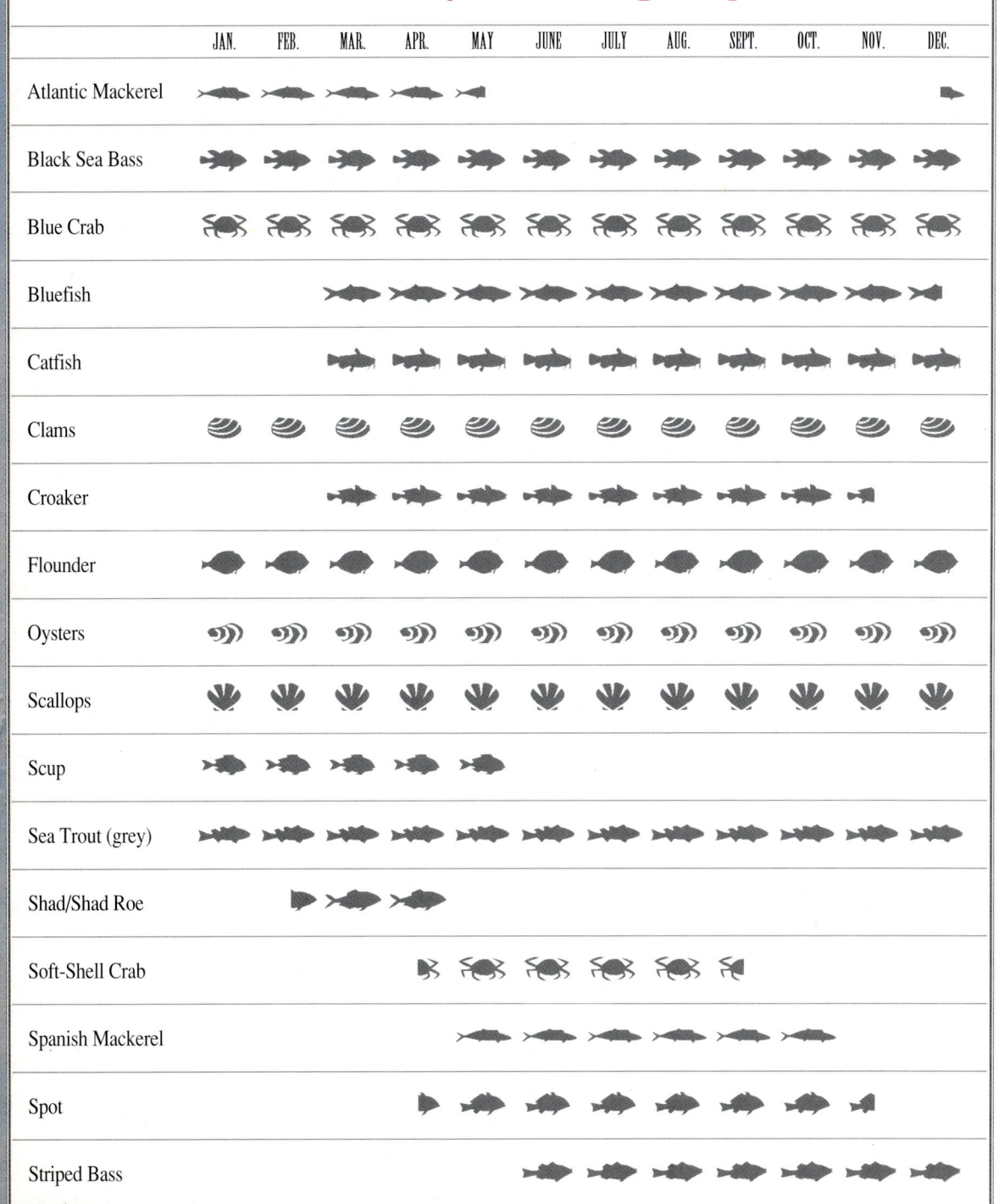

	JAN.	FEB.	MAR.	APR.	MAY	JUNE	JULY	AUG.	SEPT.	OCT.	NOV.	DEC.
Atlantic Mackerel	●	●	●	●	●							●
Black Sea Bass	●	●	●	●	●	●	●	●	●	●	●	●
Blue Crab	●	●	●	●	●	●	●	●	●	●	●	●
Bluefish				●	●	●	●	●	●	●	●	●
Catfish				●	●	●	●	●	●	●	●	●
Clams	●	●	●	●	●	●	●	●	●	●	●	●
Croaker				●	●	●	●	●	●	●	●	
Flounder	●	●	●	●	●	●	●	●	●	●	●	●
Oysters	●	●	●	●	●	●	●	●	●	●	●	●
Scallops	●	●	●	●	●	●	●	●	●	●	●	●
Scup	●	●	●	●	●							
Sea Trout (grey)	●	●	●	●	●	●	●	●	●	●	●	●
Shad/Shad Roe			●	●	●							
Soft-Shell Crab					●	●	●	●	●	●		
Spanish Mackerel					●	●	●	●	●	●		
Spot					●	●	●	●	●	●	●	
Striped Bass						●	●	●	●	●	●	●

Frozen Available Year-Round

Grilled Oriental Croaker/Spot

4 large dressed spot (or medium croaker or black sea bass)	2 tablespoons orange peel, finely julienned
¼ cup soy sauce	2 tablespoons orange juice
2 tablespoons brown sugar	¼ teaspoon red pepper flakes, crushed
1 clove garlic, minced	2 tablespoons butter, melted
1 tablespoon fresh ginger, minced	4 scallions, sliced

Place fish in a bowl. Combine remaining ingredients and pour over fish. Marinate one hour. • Place fish on a grill, about 5 inches from heat for about 10 minutes per inch thickness of fish, turning once half-way through cooking time and basting often with the marinade. When fish is tender and flakes easily, remove from grill and serve hot. • Fish can also be cooked indoors by placing it on a broiler pan and broiling about 5 inches from the heat for 10 minutes per inch of thickness, turning once half-way through the process. Serves 4. *Pictured at left.*

Total calories per serving: 335 • Percentage of calories from protein: 46 • Percentage of calories from carbohydrates: 14 Percentage of calories from fat: 38 • Percentage of calories from saturated fat: 14

Spicy Pan-Fried Croaker

3 pounds croaker, cleaned	¼ teaspoon dry mustard
1 cup yellow cornmeal	¼ teaspoon onion powder
1½ teaspoons paprika	1 cup milk
1 teaspoon salt	bacon fat for frying*
½ teaspoon celery salt	lemon wedges for garnish
½ teaspoon pepper	

Wash fish and pat dry. Combine cornmeal and seasonings. Dip fish in milk and then roll in seasoned cornmeal. Place fish in a single layer in hot bacon fat in a 12-inch skillet. Fry at a moderate heat for 4 to 5 minutes or until brown. Turn carefully. Fry 4 to 5 minutes longer or until fish are brown and flake easily when tested with a fork. Drain on absorbent paper. Serve with lemon wedges. *Serves 6.*

*or substitute your favorite oil

Total calories per serving: 370 • Percentage of calories from protein: 41 • Percentage of calories from carbohydrates: 3 Percentage of calories from fat: 54 • Percentage of calories from saturated fat: 18

Virginia Croaker With Brown Potatoes And Sausage Butter
Chef J. David Everett, C.E.C., The Dining Room At Ford's Colony, Williamsburg

4 croakers, cleaned with skin on
   sea salt, to taste
   freshly ground black pepper, to taste
4 sprigs fresh rosemary
12 small new potatoes, sliced and browned in olive oil

Sausage Butter

2 ounces fresh sausage
1 clove shallot
½ clove garlic
1 tablespoon fresh chives
1 tablespoon fresh chervil
1 tablespoon fresh parsley
   sea salt, to taste
   pepper, freshly ground, to taste
1 ounce white wine
½ ounce fish stock
½ ounce heavy cream
2 ounces whole butter, softenened

Rub fish with olive oil and season with salt, pepper and sprigs of rosemary. Cover well and refrigerate until ready to cook. • Remove herb and place skin side up under broiler or in oven just long enough to cook, 2 to 3 minutes. Place on Sausage Butter and serve with browned small new potatoes. Serves 4.

Sauté herbs, shallot, garlic and sausage in the fat released from the sausage. • Add white wine and reduce by half. Bring fish stock and cream to a boil; remove from heat. Whip butter into the liquid, stir continually, so the sauce will not separate.

Total calories per serving: 515
Percentage of calories from protein: 32
Percentage of calories from carbohydrates: 36
Percentage of calories from fat: 29
Percentage of calories from saturated fat: 12

Anyone who has ever caught a croaker, knows how it got its name. But no one really knows why the "talking fish" talks - whether to keep in touch with other members of the school, to echo sounds for depth or to express itself during breeding season. Its loud and distinctive "voice" did manage to foil the U.S. Government and scientists during WWII when a hydrophone system set up in the Chesapeake Bay to detect German submarines began to pick up incessant signals - as it turned out, the call of the croaker. This is no idle chatter!